Hurricanes

Hurricanes

Peter Murray

THE CHILD'S WORLD, INC.

Library of Congress Cataloging-in-Publication Data
Murray, Peter, 1952 Sept. 29–
Hurricanes / by Peter Murray.
p.   cm.
Includes index.
Summary: Using Hurricane Andrew as an example,
describes the formation, course, and effects
of these violent storms and explains how
scientists predict and track them.
ISBN 1-56766-547-0 (library reinforced : alk paper)
1. Hurricanes—Juvenile literature.
[1. Hurricane Andrew, 1992. 2. Hurricanes]   I. Title.
QC944.2.M87   1998
551.55'2—dc21   98-3256
CIP
AC

Photo Credits

© Alan Klehr/Tony Stone Images: 24
© Arnulf Husmo/Tony Stone Images: 2
© Art Wolfe/Tony Stone Images: 20
© IS Ltd./Tony Stone Worldwide: 6
© 1992 J. Christopher/Weatherstock: 29
© Ken Biggs/Tony Stone Images: cover
© 1996 M. Laca/Weatherstock: 26
© Norman O. Tomalin/Bruce Coleman, Inc.: 23
© Peter LeGrand/Ton Stone Images: 13
© Rex Ziak/Tony Stone Images: 10
© 1992 Warren Faidley/Weatherstock: 19
© Warren Faidley/Weatherstock: 15, 30
© Weatherstock/NOAA: 9, 16

On the cover...

Front cover: This strong hurricane is pushing waves onto a beach.
Page 2: A hurricane's winds are creating these rough waves.

Table of Contents

Chapter	Page
Hurricane!	7
How Do We Learn About Hurricanes?	8
What Is a Hurricane Watch?	11
Are All Hurricanes Alike?	12
How Do Hurricanes Form?	14
Can We Tell Where a Hurricane Will Go?	18
What Is a Hurricane Warning?	21
What Should You Do to Stay Safe?	22
What Is a Storm Surge?	27
Do Hurricanes Cause Damage?	28
Index & Glossary	32

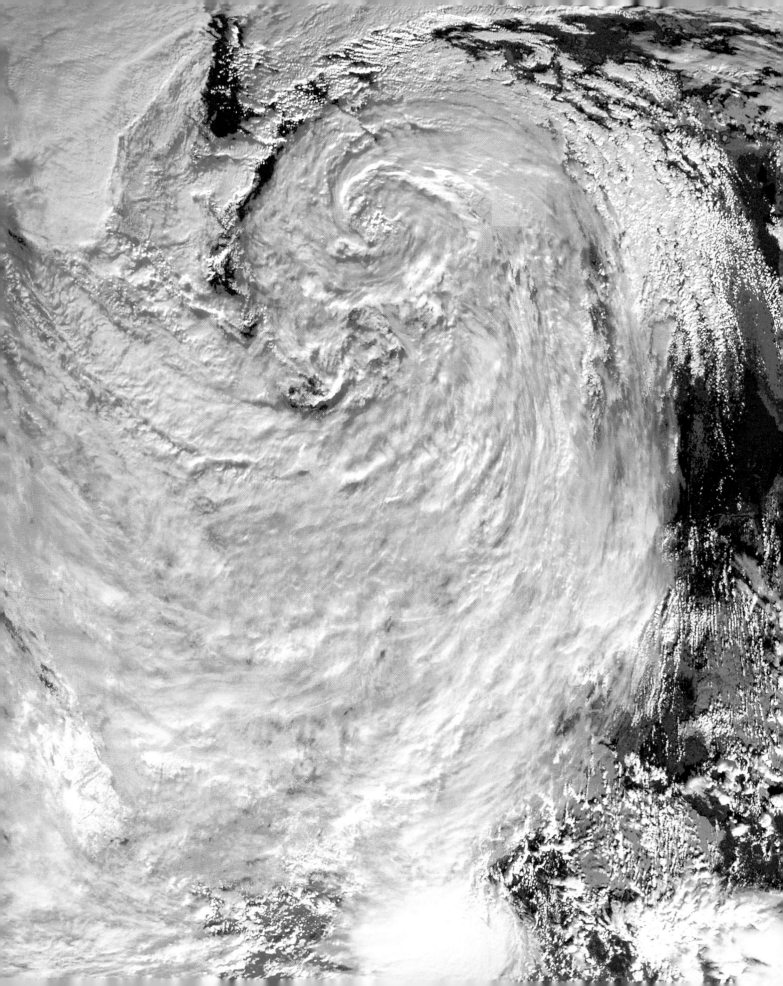

It is a hot August day in Florida. But in outer space, a weather satellite detects something strange over the Atlantic Ocean. Some clouds are circling around, forming an enormous pinwheel hundreds of miles across. The satellite takes photographs and sends them to the National Hurricane Center in Florida.

Weather scientists, called **meteorologists**, look at the pictures. They give the area of swirling clouds a name. They call it Tropical Storm Andrew.

← These swirling clouds are forming a tropical storm.

How Do We Learn About Hurricanes?

The storm is still very far away, but the next photos show that it is moving toward the United States. The scientists decide to send out a plane called a *Hurricane Hunter.* The plane will take a closer look at the approaching storm.

The airplane is designed to fly in the roughest weather. Even so, the trip is dangerous. The Hurricane Hunter flies directly into the clouds. Its instruments measure the size, speed, direction, and force of the swirling clouds. The Hurricane Hunter radios its findings back to the Hurricane Center.

This Hurricane Hunter is getting ready to fly into a storm. ⇒

What Is a Hurricane Watch?

The meteorologists are alarmed by the report. The winds of the storm have risen to over 100 miles per hour! They give Tropical Storm Andrew a new name. They now call it Hurricane Andrew.

They also broadcast a **hurricane watch** for the southeast coast. A watch means that a hurricane has formed over the ocean. There is a chance that the storm will reach the coast within two days.

⇐ This tropical storm is turning into a hurricane.

Are All Hurricanes Alike?

Scientists who study hurricanes rate them by measuring their wind speeds. *Category 1 hurricanes* have winds of 74 to 95 miles per hour. That's enough to blow the leaves off trees. *Category 5* hurricanes are the most powerful. They have winds over 200 miles per hour. That's strong enough to tear up trees by their roots and bend lampposts to the ground!

A Category 5 hurricane tipped this tree over onto a house. ⇒

How Do Hurricanes Form?

Hurricanes form mostly during the warmer months of the year. During warm weather, the sun heats the ocean's surface all day long. Some of the water changes into a mist called **water vapor**. The warm water vapor rises high into the air. As it does, cooler air rushes in to replace it. This causes winds to form.

These clouds are full of rising water vapor. ⇒

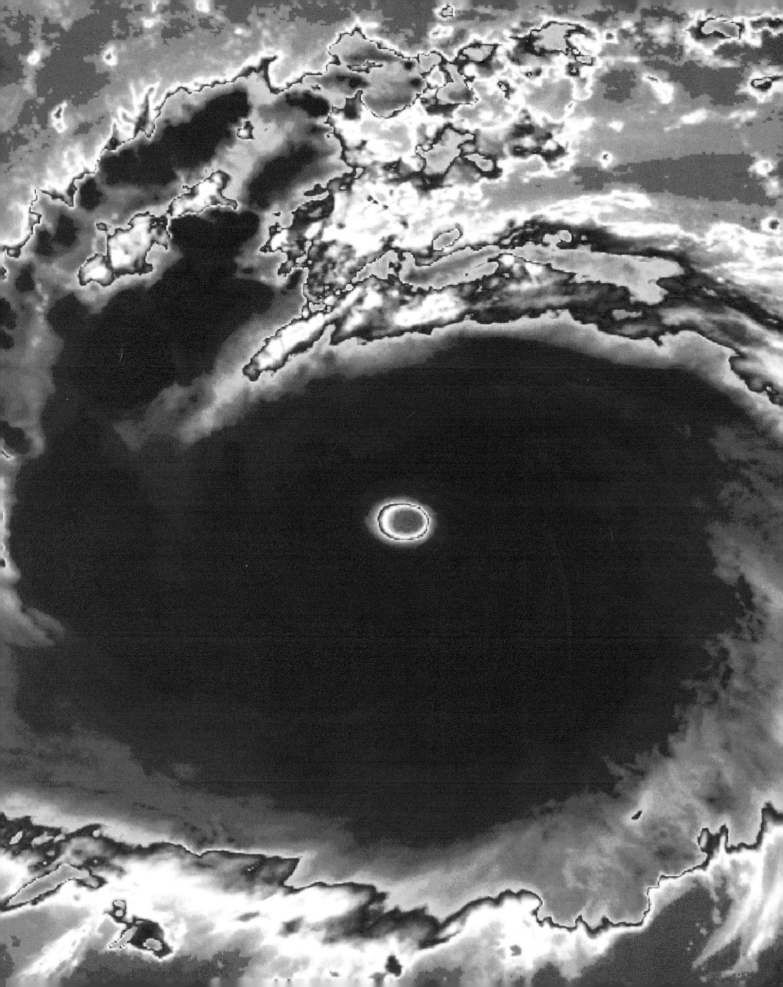

When conditions are right, the rising water vapor forms into clouds. The winds swirl the clouds into a huge doughnut shape hundreds of miles across. The clouds on the outside of the "doughnut" bring strong winds and very heavy rains. But the middle of the hurricane is peaceful.

The middle of a hurricane is called the **eye**. In the eye, the winds are calm and the weather is quiet. In fact, if you were in the eye of a hurricane, you could look straight up and see blue sky!

Can We Tell Where a Hurricane Will Go?

Back in Florida, the giant, spinning storm known as Hurricane Andrew is moving closer to the coast. Meteorologists want to know if it is coming to their area. They use computers to map the path of the hurricane and try to figure out where it will go. Sometimes the meteorologists can tell where a hurricane will go. Other times, the hurricane fools everyone and changes direction.

This computer screen shows how close the hurricane is to Florida. ⇒

What Is a Hurricane Warning?

As it gets closer, the hurricane grows in strength. The winds are now swirling at 150 miles per hour. According to the computers, Andrew will reach South Florida within 24 hours. The National Hurricane Center issues a **hurricane warning**. The warning tells people to leave the area until the storm is over.

What Should You Do to Stay Safe?

If there is a hurricane warning for the area where you live, you should take it very seriously. Board up all the windows in your home to keep them from breaking. Bring your lawn furniture and yard toys inside so they don't blow away in the strong winds. Most important, you and your family should get in your car and drive inland to wait out the storm.

These windows have been taped to keep them from breaking. ⇒

As Hurricane Andrew approaches the coast of Florida, the sky grows very dark. Rain begins to fall and the winds pick up. Soon the wind is blowing so hard that the raindrops seem to be going sideways! Tree branches and roof shingles tumble through the air. The sewers back up, flooding the streets. But the worst part of the storm is yet to come!

What Is a Storm Surge?

The worst hurricane damage isn't caused by the wind and rain. The strong **storm surge** is the most dangerous part. As a hurricane nears land, the wind pushes a mound of water ahead of the storm. This raises the level of the ocean as much as 20 feet. The huge wall of water moves quickly toward land. When it finally crashes onto the shore, it destroys everything in its path. Imagine a wall of water as high as your house!

⇐ This hurricane is pushing huge waves onto the shore.

Do Hurricanes Cause Damage?

Hurricane Andrew's storm surge and winds destroy 63,000 homes in Florida before the storm finally moves on. The next day, Andrew crashes onto the coast of Louisiana, destroying more homes and businesses.

As it moves inland, Hurricane Andrew loses its power. Without the warm waters of the ocean to create its swirling winds, the storm calms down. By the time Andrew reaches northern Mississippi, it is just another rainstorm.

Hurricane Andrew destroyed these trailer homes in Florida. ⇒

Hurricanes are very dangerous storms. But even though we cannot stop them from happening, we can learn when and where they will strike. With the help of satellites, weather planes, computers, and meteorologists, we can understand more about these strong storms and how to protect ourselves from them.

Glossary

eye (EYE)
The hole in the middle of a hurricane is called the eye. The weather in the eye is calm.

hurricane warning (HUR–ih–kane WAR–ning)
A hurricane warning means that a hurricane will move into an area. The warning lets people know that they should leave the area until the storm is over.

hurricane watch (HUR–ih–kane WATCH)
A hurricane watch means that there is a hurricane over the ocean. The watch tells people that the hurricane might move toward them.

meteorologists (mee–tee–yor–AH–luh–jists)
Meteorologists are scientists who study the weather. They try to predict where hurricanes will go.

storm surge (STORM SURJ)
A storm surge is a huge wall of water pushed by the hurricane. Storm surges are dangerous and can cause lots of damage when they hit the shore.

Index

damage, 27, 28

different kinds, 12

eye, 17

formation, 7, 14, 17

Hurricane Hunter, 8

hurricane warning, 21-22

hurricane watch, 11

meteorologists, 7, 11, 18, 31

rain, 25

safety tips, 22

storm surge, 27-28

National Hurricane Center, 7, 8, 21

water vapor, 14, 17

winds, 25, 28